PTA Fundraising

Uniform Sales

Anne Dunn

Also available from this Author:

PTA Fundraising

Copyright © 2017 Anne Dunn

All rights reserved.

ISBN-13: 978-1545231401

ISBN-10: 1545231400

CONTENTS

	Introduction	i
1	Why have a Uniform Sale	1
2	Having a Uniform Sale	11
3	Having a Uniform Sale- What you'll need	17
4	Task Checklist	19
5	Volunteer Schedule	25
6	Sample Documents	26
7	After the Event	29

Introduction

This book is a step by step guide for PTAs who are considering starting to do Uniform Sales. It explains the benefits of Uniform Sales and gives detailed advice on how to set up and run one from start to finish.

Uniform sales are a great way to for PTAs to raise money without having a large outlay to set up the event, have the potential to raise a large amount of money and benefit the children and families of the school.

1 WHY HAVE A UNIFORM SALE

<u>Why do Uniform Sales?</u>

PTAs should always be looking out for new fundraising activities. Out of all the possible fundraising activities that PTAs can do, Uniform Sales are a particularly attractive idea. As well as being a potentially lucrative fundraiser they can also offer various other benefits to the PTA and the school community.

<u>Benefits of a Uniform Sale</u>

Potential to be a lucrative fundraiser

> What do all Parents need?
>
> What do many Parents give away?
>
> **School Uniform!**

All parents of children at school need to ensure that their children have the correct School Uniform. As children outgrow uniform, many parents give the uniform away. If the PTA can encourage the parents to donate unwanted uniform to them, then they can sell the uniform on at minimal cost as the "stock" has all been donated. This means that profit margins could be higher than many other fundraisers as the core stock has not cost anything to buy.

Gives parents somewhere to dispose of unwanted uniform

Children outgrow their uniform quickly! Some parents are better than others at taking unwanted clothes to the charity shop. Many parents will appreciate the opportunity to be able to drop unwanted uniform off at school so that they do not have the old uniform taking up space at home. Dropping it off at school means not having to make a special trip out to the charity shop for many people. Because some parents will be pleased to be able to dispose of the unwanted uniform without having to make an extra trip to the charity shop, they should be happy to donate to school as it saves them a trip and valuable time. Generally, people would rather donate and see the clothes being of use than throwing them away. Although some parents will have younger siblings who can use the uniform, many others do not and will therefore need to dispose of it to make room for their child's new uniform as they grow.

If you feel that parents at your school may need extra encouragement to donate you could offer them an incentive for doing so such as:

- A pass to get into the sale 15 minutes earlier than everyone else
- A discount voucher off their total spend on uniform sold by the PTA- up to 25% would still keep it profitable and could really boost donations and therefore stock you have to sell.

Can be a real benefit to lower income families who struggle with the cost of buying new school uniform

Saving money on the cost of purchasing school uniform is helpful to everybody as it is expensive. But to lower income families, it can make a huge difference to their family finances. Many families really worry about how they will pay for the new uniform each year, and particularly as their child first starts a new school when they have to be fully kitted out with everything new. This can be a significant cost to some families and the opportunity to purchase at least some of it at a reduced rate will reduce their stress in finding the money. This can only be beneficial to the children in the family so is a tangible benefit to the school community as well as raising funds for the PTA.

Easy to collect

Many PTAs participate in clothes recycling schemes as a fundraising activity. This means that parents are already accustomed to collecting unwanted clothes and donating them to school. If your PTA already does this, then your parents should be more willing to donate uniform because they are already used to sorting and bringing unwanted clothes to school when the PTA asks them to.

Many of the recycling schemes have a list of items they cannot accept, and most of these specify school uniform with logos. If this is the case for your recycling scheme, then you do not have the worry that you are reducing the amount that this raises because much of the uniform wouldn't be suitable for the collection anyway. The items that you could have used for recycling (e.g. plain shirts etc.) will raise more money sold individually than as part of the recycling. You could tie in your uniform collection with the next clothes for recycling collection by asking parents to separate out uniform from everything else and having a separate collection area for it.

If you don't currently participate in a clothes recycling scheme, they are an excellent way of raising money. They are comparatively low effort as parents are asked to bring their donations to school on the same day as the recycling company collects them so there is no worry about having to store them in the meantime. Some PTAs do have the facility to store donations made in between collections, and there is no doubt that this will increase the amount collected, but the event can be successfully run by just asking for donations on the day.

Alternatively, if you don't currently run a recycling scheme, you could start off with collecting Uniform. Once you have the parents accustomed to donating items of Uniform, you could then start running a recycling scheme in tandem with the Uniform collections and ask parents to separate Uniform from everything else.

Great way for new families to meet their PTA

What better way for new families to meet their PTA than at an event that is saving them money?! They will benefit from saving money by buying the uniform and at the same time meet PTA volunteers in a positive, friendly environment. Provided the PTA tells parents how much the event has raised afterwards, they will also feel that they helped the school by participating in the event which is a great start to their relationship with the PTA. This will make a great first impression of the PTA to new families and make them much more likely to either participate in future events, or even better volunteer to help with them. They will have already met the PTA volunteers that ran the Uniform Sale which means they may be more likely to come to PTA meetings, rather than feeling nervous that they won't know anybody there.

This is why having a Uniform Sale at the new parents' induction evening is such a good idea. Hopefully your school will be easily persuaded as the event will be raising money for the school and they will see the value of getting new parents "on side" with the PTA so early on in their child's school career. It also means that parents will get to see what the correct uniform is so their children are more likely to be wearing the right clothes when they start at the school. This helps school because staff won't have to enforce the uniform policy (some schools are very strict) which saves them time, and helps them build positive relationships with the parents of the new children that year.

Other fundraising can be done at the same time

If your Uniform Sales are a success and you decide to run them more often than just for new parents, such as for the whole school, then you have the opportunity to add other ways of fundraising to the event. The most obvious one is serving light refreshments at the Uniform Sale. Tea, coffee, soft drinks and maybe biscuits, cakes and snacks are all easy to do but potentially profitable. As they cost so little to put on, you can sell them cheaply and still make a profit on them. Having refreshments available could also encourage people to stay longer and potentially spend more money whilst they are at the sale. Refreshments will also give the event a more social feel which makes it more enjoyable for everyone there. If parents enjoy the Uniform Sale AND get to save money then hopefully it will become a very popular event at the school.

You could then consider expanding your "range" of products beyond the donated uniform. Is there a list of equipment that children must take to school? If they have to have say certain pens, pencils or other stationary equipment could the PTA source these products to buy wholesale and sell at the event? If bought wholesale, the PTA may be able to sell them at a price that saves parents money whilst still making a profit and raising funds.

If you are a large school with particular sporting items and equipment that are needed, could you do a deal with a local sports equipment shop? This may be easier to do if you have a number of similar shops who would all be eager to get the sales from a school's worth of children buying the equipment as this would provide a greater incentive for a particular shop to want to support the event and get the opportunity to take orders from parents. Maybe they could have a stand at the sale and offer items on a special sale night price, or issue a discount voucher to parents who attend the sale to use at the shop on another day. They may be happy to do this in order to secure the custom from your school's families. You could offer to display their logo on the fliers you send to parents informing them of the sale. Maybe you could push for a "sponsorship" of the event by the shop where they give a discount to parents at the sale and via the voucher later on, and pay the PTA either a small element of commission or a set amount to have their stand at your event.

This will help the PTA because as well as the obvious commission or money paid for the stall, it could be a valuable incentive for parents to attend the sale. The opportunity to obtain a discount for parents that attend the sale – either by purchasing from the external company on the night, or by using a voucher they get on the night would encourage parents to attend the Uniform Sale as they could save more money on the cost of kitting their child out for school.

If you decide to organise an event like this, the PTA could be helping the school's families by saving them money on the costs of the uniform, stationary and sporting equipment, whilst at the same time raising money on all of these products as well as from the refreshment sales at the event. Even at a small school, as well as for the non-monetary benefits already mentioned, this type of event has the potential to raise a worthwhile amount of money. A large school with several hundred families attending would mean a larger sale so a large event to organise, but with the potential to raise a significant amount of money for the PTA.

Another fundraiser that could easily be added to a Uniform Sale is a raffle. Tickets could be sold at the event, with the tickets being drawn on the night. If you had a number of external companies at the event, you could ask them to donate a raffle prize as part of their fee for attending the event.

Increasing attendance at other events

If you find your Uniform Sales are popular, but perhaps not to the scale suggested above where you have a large event with a range of products and suppliers available, you could consider adding it onto another PTA event. Many PTAs feel they could improve attendance at large events such as Summer Fairs. Incorporating the Uniform Sale into an event like this is worth considering as it could bring parents who wouldn't normally attend to the event. When they are there, they may end up participating in other areas of the event in addition to the Uniform Sale. This would then boost the amount that the rest of the event raised due to the increased number of people attending, even if they didn't go round all of the stalls.

School concerns

Some, but not all, schools make commission from the uniform they sell directly to parents, or from certain suppliers so may have reservations about the PTA selling second hand uniform. Remind them of all the other benefits that the uniform sales will bring to the school community- as well as the money raised for the PTA (which of course is spent on the school and it's pupils). Also remind them that not all parents will donate uniform for whatever reasons, and not all of the uniform donated will be of sufficient quality to sell. Therefore there will still be a need for new uniform. The school will not lose out on revenue it gains from the sale of new uniform by too much, and whatever reduction there is will be more than outweighed by the money raised by the PTA in doing the sale and the other benefits to the school community.

2 HAVING A UNIFORM SALE

If you have decided you would like to run a Uniform Sale you will need certain resources in order to do so and various tasks to be done along the way to make the event run smoothly.

You will need:

<u>Volunteers</u>
As ever for PTA events, you will need volunteers! So one of the first things you will need to do once you have decided to run a Uniform Sale is to recruit some volunteers. Uniform sales do involve a few stages in the process, so have quite a high volunteer requirement. However perhaps allowing volunteers access to the Uniform on sale for half an hour before it opens to everyone else, or a similar incentive, would encourage people to help out. Different volunteers can do different parts of the process so people could be asked to help with specific tasks with only a few key volunteers involved from start to finish. As with all PTA Events, make sure you thank your volunteers afterwards to ensure they feel appreciated and therefore more likely to help again in the future.

(See separate volunteer schedule which identifies specific tasks that you will need volunteers for.)

Having a Uniform Sale

Running a Uniform Sale will involve a number of tasks from planning the event, to sourcing and processing the stock to running the Sale on the day and afterwards.

-Planning the event-
- The type of event- choose the scale to suit you. Anything from one table at the new parents' induction to a large event for all school parents to attend. Perhaps start with a small event first and take it from there.
- Date (are you doing a small sale at the new parents' induction, or a larger standalone event, or tagging onto another existing event)
- What will your Uniform sale consist of- just the PTA selling clothes or will the PTA also sell other supplies? Will you be inviting other retailers to participate in the event in return for offering a discount and "sponsorship" of the event.
- Will you be offering refreshments at the event? If so what and who will run that side of it?
- Venue- where will you hold your Uniform Sale? If you are running your Uniform Sale for new parents at the new parents' induction, you will need to hold it where that is. Depending on the size of school, and therefore the number of new parents

there are likely to be at the event, you could have a table in the room where the induction event is being held, a classroom or the school hall. If you are running the Uniform Sale as part of a larger event such as a Fair then you will need to consider how to accommodate the Uniform Sale within the larger event.

- o Outside Organisations:
    - Will you invite some to participate in the event?
    - How many? What sort?
    - Pricing- What will they pay to attend?
        - Flat rate for stall?
        - Commission?
        - Raffle prize?
- o Raffle:
    - Will you have one?
    - What prizes will you use?
    - How much will you charge for tickets?
    - One big bumper prize of all the items donated or a few smaller prizes?

- *Organising the clothes collection*
  This will include notifying parents to encourage as many donations as possible. Consider what if any incentives could be offered to parents who donate so details can be put on the information sent out to encourage more donations. This will also mean arranging what will happen on the day that parents bring the clothes, and where the collection point is at school. Make sure that this is all organised with the school prior to sending out the fliers to prevent confusion later on.

- *Storage*
  This will mean ensuring that the clothes are stored properly from when they are collected to when they are sold. This could include:

    o Arranging storage for the clothes collected
    o Storage of the clothes throughout the process between collection and the Sale.
    o Having storage available for any items that are left over from the sale- either until the next sale or until they can be disposed of.

- *Processing clothes*
  This will entail:

    o Going through the clothes collected and removing clothes that aren't in very good or almost new condition.
    o Sorting into different types of clothes
    o Sorting each types of clothes into sizes
    o Washing and drying the clothes
    o Folding or ironing

  Is there a local launderette near the school? Could they be persuaded to do some of the washing and drying in return for being a named "sponsor" on the fliers for the event? This would save an awful lot of work for the PTA, and give the laundry the opportunity for many people to see what a good job they do. Launderettes have industrial washers and driers so could get through a large quantity of clothes in only a few loads.

  Maybe all the clothes could have a "laundered by x launderette" sticker on them. Laundering the clothes seems like more work, but people will be much more inclined to buy if they can see all the uniform on sale is in good condition, clean and ready to use- and they will pay more for it. Remember you are selling an alternative to people buying new uniform- albeit at a bargain price but you still want people to feel they are getting something worth having that they are happy for their child to wear. If they feel that what you are selling is of low quality, many people will not buy it, however cheap it is. Ensure your uniform sales get the reputation for only selling good quality items and they will be very popular.

3 HAVING A UNIFORM SALE- WHAT YOU'LL NEED

The list below gives a starting point for the supplies that you will need to run a Uniform Sale. You may find you don't need all of them, or that there are other things that would be useful but this list will should help start you off.

- Washing powder
- Fabric conditioner (if required)
- Labels / stickers – for sizes and prices
- Pens- for labelling
- Clothes Hangers
- Hanging Rails
- Table to display folded items
- Float on the day (from your Treasurer)
- Large paper for posters to show prices on the day
- Bags for people to take their purchases away in. Either traditional carrier bags, or you could investigate if you could get printed canvas bags at a low enough cost to sell or giveaway with a certain spend. This would have the benefit of parents having a PTA branded item that they are likely to reuse- which will remind them about the PTA and perhaps encourage them to support future events.

Storage

You will need somewhere to store the uniform once collected, and then during and after processing. Hopefully after the sale you will have sold most of your stock, but you may be left with some uniform which can be saved until the next uniform sale. Always worth asking school if they might have a cupboard somewhere that could be used, or dividing the clothes amongst a number of volunteers so that no one person has to find room for a large quantity of clothes.

Refreshments

If you are running a refreshment stall, you would also need to plan for that and the supplies that will be needed. This should be straightforward to most PTAs as many run refreshment stalls at a variety of events throughout the year.

Raffle

If you are running a raffle you will need prizes, tickets and someone to sell tickets. As with refreshments, raffles are something most PTAs run frequently so should be straightforward.

4 UNIFORM SALE TASK CHECKLIST

This chapter is a checklist for tasks that will need to be done as part of running a Uniform Sale, as well as a Volunteer Schedule to organize your volunteers and ensure that volunteers are arranged for all tasks associated with running a Uniform Sale. You can use this as a starting point when doing the checklist for your Uniform Sale.

Checklist

Task	Done	Who
Decide the type of Uniform Sale you are running- Small for New Parents or Large for whole school		
Recruit enough volunteers for your event to ensure it can run (see separate volunteer schedule)		
Confirm venue and date with school		
Arrange for school to send out information about the Uniform Sale to new parents – get deadline for information to be provided to them to be sent out (if you can arrange for clothes collection to be before this you can always cancel in the unlikely event of insufficient donations before anything has been sent to new parents and this will give plenty of time to process the donations)		

Task	Done	Who
Confirm details of clothes collection- date / drop off point for donated clothes		
Create fliers to send out to parents asking for donations (if Uniform Sale for new parents only you only need to ask parents of the youngest year groups- if Uniform Sale for all parents you will need to ask them all). Ensure flier has full details of date, drop off point and any incentive you are offering for donations.		
Social media – to remind parents to donate clothing, and to remind parents to attend the Uniform Sale (if not just for New Parents). And for posting the total amount raised as soon as possible after the event.		
Publicity for Uniform Sale – fliers to parents informing of date and time and giving details of savings that can be made to encourage attendance (see separate sample flier)		

Task	Done	Who
Donated stock: - Arrange suitable storage for immediately after donation - Process all donated clothes - Arrange suitable storing for clothes once processed (may be different to prior to processing if things now need to be stored hung up on rails or folded) - Decide pricing in advance so that details of amount parents can save on new uniform costs can be put onto the flier that goes out to inform them of the Uniform Sale - Arrange for it to be transported to Venue in good time for Uniform Sale - Arrange for longer term storage of any left over stock until either disposed of or until the next Uniform Sale.		
Ensuring all stock has been processed and priced. Consider cataloguing what you have to look at sales after the event to identify what items sell well for next time.		

Task	Done	Who
Working with Outside Organisations (if you have decided to involve some) - Approaching Organisations with information about the event - Adding their information to your publicity flier if agreed - Taking bookings and payments - Ensuring their stall / table at the event is as agreed with them - Ensuring they are looked after on the day so have everything they need (they are paying to be there so keep them happy) - If they are paying commission on their sales at the event, ensure that you know how much they owe and get this as soon as possible from them.		
Refreshments: - Adapt the checklist you would usually use for running refreshments at PTA events		

Task	Done	Who
Venue: - Planning and set up before the Uniform Sale - Creation of notices to display prices of the different items - Ensuring all stock is displayed properly at the sale (e.g. set out in sizes, some on tables some on hangers dependent on the item) - Ensuring all running smoothly during the sale - Clearing up and removing equipment and left over stock after the Sale		
Raffle: - Get tickets - Collect prize donations - Publicise (you could put on the event flier) - Sell tickets on day - Remember to draw the raffle on the day!		

Task	Done	Who
Money: - Provide floats with adequate change - Collect money in immediately after the sale and count quickly so that a total raised can be announced within a day or two. - Bank money as soon as possible		
Ensure that all volunteers are thanked for helping out at the Uniform Sale		

4 VOLUNTEER SCHEDULE

Task	Who
Recruit enough volunteers for your event to ensure it can run	
Overall running and overseeing of event from start to finish	
Volunteer to confirm dates with school and to ensure all information sent out in time	
Volunteer to create fliers	
Volunteers for collection day	
Volunteers to process the stock	
Volunteer to deal with social media	
Volunteers to organize and run the event itself (see Task Checklist for more detail on tasks which will need volunteers)	
Volunteer to deal with the money- providing float, providing a total figure raised for the event and ensuring the money is banked as soon as possible after the event. (Likely to be your Treasurer)	

5 SAMPLE DOCUMENTS

Flier to ask for Donations

UNIFORM WANTED!

6th May

We need your outgrown and surplus Uniform as we will be running a Uniform Sale in aid of the PTA.

Any donations of good condition Uniform Items will be much appreciated.
As a thank you, everyone who donates Uniform will receive a voucher that will get them 15% off at the Uniform Sale.

Please drop items off at the main school gate on 6th May

X SCHOOL PTA

Voucher for those that Donate

Thank you for your donation to our Uniform Sale!

This voucher entitles you to 15% off your spend on School Uniform at the Uniform Sale

15% OFF

Please ensure that you present this voucher when you make your purchase.
Vouchers can only be used once.
You need to have the voucher with you to claim your discount.

Sample Flier to send out
(no currency specified- put the one for your country)

UNIFORM SALE!

-X School PTA is having a Uniform Sale- Save a fortune on the price of new Uniform for next year!

	Uniform Cost		Saving
	New	Our Price	
Blazer	40	15	25
Trousers / Skirt	15	4	11
School Jumper	15	4	11
Shirts	12 for two	3 for two	9
PE Top	10	2.50	7.50
Total	92	28.50	63.50

You could make a total saving of 63.50

Join us at X Place on X Date and X Time for our Uniform Sale to make huge savings on the cost of Uniform and help raise funds for the PTA.

All clothing is of good usable quality and is freshly laundered.

Light refreshments will be available.

Enter our Raffle to WIN a fabulous prize!

6 AFTER THE EVENT

If you had a Uniform Sale, hopefully it was a successful event that you would like to run again. It is always worth reviewing an event soon after having it so that you can identify any areas which you might like to change for the next time you do it. The following few questions are a starting point. The sooner you consider these after the event the better, as it will be fresh in your mind.

Event name:

How much did it raise:

What went well with the event?

What could have gone better?

Are there any elements of the event that we would prefer not to do next time?

Is there anything that we would like to add to this event next time we have it?

What do we need to remember for next time we hold this event?

Who volunteered this time? (so you remember who knows how to do it for next time)

ABOUT THE AUTHOR

The author has been extensively involved with PTAs for nearly ten years. This included a four year term as Treasurer as well as time doing the work of the Secretary and Chair roles. This has given her wide experience of the mechanics of fundraising events for the PTA.

Anne has a real understanding of challenges that PTAs can face in terms of engagement with parents and finding and keeping volunteers as well as being passionate about fundraising for PTAs and other good causes.

Follow Anne for fundraising tips and news about forthcoming books at:

- Twitter at @PTAFundraising
- Facebook PTA Fundraising

www.ingramcontent.com/pod-product-compliance
Lightning Source LLC
Chambersburg PA
CBHW061235180526
45170CB00003B/1302